A Beginners' Handboc   **al**
Tips and Advice for Ne

John C. Dunn

Copyright © 2015 by John C. Dunn

Find us on the web at Dunnconsultingservices.com

ISBN 13: 978-1507668856

ISBN 10: 1507668856

Notice of rights

Acknowledgement

The author would like to thank the following people whom without their ongoing support this book would not have been possible. Anne-Marie Laberge, Todd Charlebois, Sarah Hickson.

National Library of Canada Cataloging in Publication Data

Bibliothéque nationale du Québec

Library of Congress Cataloging in Publication Data

Table of Contents

Introduction

A Beginner's Handbook for Hospitality Sales was created to give sales executives entering the hospitality industry a quick introduction to what is expected of them, and how to successfully navigate this exciting new career environment. This handbook serves as a "crash course" in hospitality sales, providing friendly advice and helpful hints as well as detailing landmines to avoid. Ultimately, it is a practical guide of how to excel in this industry - backed up with real life examples of personal successes and failures.

As a veteran of more than twenty five years in the hospitality and tourism sector, I have found that the hotel industry does an average job when preparing new sales executives in their first months of on-boarding. New sales associates generally learn "on the fly" and lack any real formal sales training until after their probationary period. Hospitality chains do have great training programs, but they are often implemented months into a new sales executive's career- impacting the sales person's ability to function properly in those first few months and potentially negatively on the business as a whole. A sales associate who is ill-prepared to face a client can translate into lost hotel revenues, and a short-lived hospitality career for that individual.

I began my journey in this business right after university, selling frozen french fries to hotels and restaurants and fighting for margins so small they only made a difference on huge bulk orders. I quickly realized that being on the other side of the equation seemed much more rewarding and enjoyable. I also realized selling was not the issue - what you sell makes all the difference. This realization quickly led me to change my career towards sales and marketing in the hotel business. Believing in a product and enjoying what you sell makes for a much more fulfilling career.

Since then, I have had the pleasure to work with some of the biggest hospitality brands in the world including Marriott, Hilton, IHG and Starwood, as well as small independent chains and hotels. I have also worked with some of the finest convention centres and convention visitors' bureaus on the continent. Along the way I have witnessed and experienced first-hand some of the largest changes and innovations within the industry and have had the good fortune to meet fascinating people, make great friends and travel the world. It is truly a wonderful industry, full of opportunity and unique experiences.

You will often hear in this business that a hotel's success is all about "Location, location, location!" That is true to some extent, however I have worked for hotels that have had a less-desirable locale yet were still very successful. The secret to a successful hotel is in part location, but more importantly is superior guest service, a clean up-to-date physical product, as well as effective presentation through the sales and marketing process. When all these elements come together effectively it makes for a winning formula.

There is one overreaching factor for personal and career success I like to share with new hospitality sales executives. **This is not just a regular nine to five job, it's a way of life**. When you truly embrace a career in hospitality sales, you become part of an industry that sells dreams, wellbeing and camaraderie. Colleagues and clients become your friends, your workdays are never the same, and your travels take you to interesting places to meet interesting people. You are exposed to a world the average person can only dream of. I have had the chance to travel the world, stay in the finest hotels, and meet fascinating people throughout my hospitality career. It has been a journey that I cherish and am truly grateful for.

As a new member of the hospitality industry it is important to understand that you are part of a much larger family. The tourism industry, of which the hotel sector is one part of, is a huge interrelated industry of dedicated service providers. The UNWTO (World Tourism Organization), in its Tourism Highlights Report 2014, estimates the tourism industry accounts for $1.4 trillion US$ in exports or 6% of global exports, in part generated by 1087 million international travellers. This is projected to grow to 1.8 billion travellers by 2030.

It is important for any new sales executive to be fully aware of his or her environment and understand the value of actively engaging with other tourism players in your city. Working as an industry, rather than as an individual entity, is more productive and competitively advantageous.

I hope the following pages will give you a strong base to begin what I believe will be an amazing journey.

Chapter One-Your First Day

The first day of any job is always a bit nerve racking. Your first day as a sales associate will most likely flow as such: You will arrive at the hotel dressed for success and be greeted by your Director of Sales (DOS). He or she will promptly walk you down to Human Resources (HR) to fill out a mountain of paper work. Following your HR introduction, you will be toured around the hotel to meet the staff, see the hotel and finally enjoy a short audience with the General Manager (GM). By then it will most likely be lunchtime and in the grand tradition of the business the entire sales team will take you to the dining room for a "meet & greet" lunch. So far the day seems to be going pretty well and you will probably feel that the hotel business is quite glamorous.

Following lunch you will be escorted back to the sales office and shown your desk. Be prepared, as most hotel sales offices are tucked away in a far corner of the hotel and given as little space as possible. This is no reflection on the importance of the Sales Department, but rather the hotel maximizing on all possible rentable space. At this point your DOS will show you your desk and make sure you get a day or two of training on the hotel Client Relations Management System (CRM). You will be told to go through and familiarize yourself with your assigned client list, as you will be calling them all by the end of the week. In the meantime, you will accompany the other sales mangers on site inspections to better understand how to sell the hotel. Listen, look and learn. This is the basis from which you can begin to develop your own selling style.

Of course, this is a generalization, but from years of experience I can attest that the hotel industry takes the on-boarding process for new sales professionals for granted, not realizing how the right start can make a powerful difference. Things have improved since my own first day many years ago, but the underlying process is still similar. Some hotels chains do a better job of the on-boarding process, but the general rule is that you should expect to fend for yourself to some degree. This handbook will help you get started on the right foot by "filling in some of the blanks" that you may experience throughout the process with useful tips I have garnered over the years. An up-front awareness of the seemingly "little things" is sometimes just as important as the grand theories you will be taught within your organization about sales and marketing.

TOP 6 TIPS – What to prepare for and accomplish on your first day:

1- Prior to your first day, ask your DOS to send you all the collateral available concerning the hotel and study it well. Research online to see what is being said on social media about the hotel (Tripadvisor, Travelocity, hotels.com, travel blogs, etc.). This will give you a better sense of the hotel's current environment and prepare you for what challenges or advantages lay ahead.

2- Physically visit a few similar hotels in the city to get a comparable.

3- Go to your hotel before you are to start in your new job and have a drink at the bar or eat in the restaurant, if applicable, or just walk around to get familiar with the ambiance, general service experience, and layout.

4- Arrive early on your first day. You want to set the right impression.

5- Make sure to do a complete Site Inspection of the hotel.

6- Make a list of questions throughout the day to go over with your DOS at the end of the day.

TOP 6 TIPS - What you should accomplish within your first week:

1- Be sure to meet all the department heads. Book a short meeting with each to find out what they do and how it interacts with the Sales Department.

2- Meet all key floor staff (banquets, front desk, food & beverage team) and begin to get to know them. You will need them in the future - so best to make friends early.

3- Ask the Director of Maintenance (DM) to do a Site Inspection with you of both the front of the house (pubic areas) and the back of the house (all private areas). This will give you a perspective on how the hotel works and the flexibility available within the hotel for special accommodations that will undoubtedly be requested by clients.

4- Make a list of questions and meet with your DOS at the end of each day, at least for the first week, and debrief.

5- Ask your DOS to review the top 20 client files in your mandate and provide a full debrief on each. (Who they are, what they do, how profitable are they to the hotel, any special requirements they may have, etc.)

6- Make sure to get a full and in-depth training on the hotel sales CRM (Client Relationship Management) system. This is one of the best early investments of your time that you can make. Really get to know the system now, rather than trying to figure it out as you go.

TOP 6 TIPS- What you should accomplish within your first 30 days:

1- Make sure to accompany your sales colleagues on client sites and/or sales calls as much as possible in the first few weeks. This will give you a good perspective on how they sell the hotel, and you can begin to adapt what works to your own style.

2- Once you have had the opportunity to tour the hotel extensively, participate in client sites and calls with your colleagues, it is time to try some role-playing exercises. Test your sales style with colleagues and the DOS. They can advise you on what works and doesn't before you go out and see clients on your own.

3- Meet your 20 best clients in person and establish a unique working rapport with each.

4- Visit your main competitive hotel properties to discern their strengths and weaknesses in comparison to your hotel.

5- Get to know your market/industry counterpart at your local CVB (Convention & Visitors Bureau)

6- Establish a solid weekly solicitation routine, and stick to it.

Chapter Two - Clients, the Cornerstone of Your Business

Clients are the bread and butter of your existence and are the lifeblood of your organization. They make it possible to run the business. Not to be melodramatic, but I cannot emphasise this point enough. In short, they, and their satisfaction is the cornerstone of the entire business. You are at their service in tandem with assuring the best interest of your hotel. It is a careful balancing act. The best clients are satisfied, repeat clients. They tend to be more loyal, cost effective to solicit, act as positive advocates for your organization and generate ongoing business. Your role is to maximize these types of clients, build upon existing successful relationships as you also develop new prospects.

Market Segments

You should be aware that the hospitality industry classifies clients into several different categories or "segments". Depending on the size of the hotel, these segments will be specifically handled by one or several sales executives. If more than one sales associate is assigned to the same segment, they are usually in charge of a client group that is divided by geographic area or by the size of the account. Not all hotels solicit all segments. In the case of smaller hotels, or those lacking meeting space or less strategically located, soliciting some segments are just not worth the investment.

The generally accepted defined segments hotels solicit are:

Corporate IT Market (individual business travellers) is generally the most common segment pursued by most, if not all, urban hotels. Sometimes negotiated by a centralized company mandate, or through a consortium third party firm (Amex, Maritz, HRG), or by individuals themselves, this is the core business segment of most urban hotels. These clients may enjoy preferred rates based on the level of business they supply to a hotel or chain. They may also have an exclusive relationship with your hotel/chain, or use a limited number of hotels in your city. Generally these clients are weekday based and do not generate many room nights over weekends. These travellers most likely hold corporate accounts and look for services such as, breakfast, a gym, free Wi-Fi and a speedy check-in/check-out process. Hotels usually covet this group of clients as they produce a steady flow of year-round business.

Selling to this segment is based on, in part, a well-developed relationship with clients, but somewhat less so than in other segments. Many of the bigger Corporate IT contracts are awarded through large national or regional

RFPs (Request for Proposal) and often rest on best price criteria with less concerns for other related benefits such as location or value added services. They also tend to be spearheaded by a national chain wide Sales Director. Hotel sales executives assigned to this segment usually work with smaller regional or local businesses that do not use national RFPs, and act as a liaison with the national chain office.

Individual Travellers are those clients who book your hotel for a multitude of reasons, business or pleasure, without any negotiated rate and may not be a regular or returning client. These clients usually book through some sort of online portal or directly with the hotel and get the rate of day. They tend to shop around to find the best available rate and will use any discounts available to them (AAA, AARP, government discounts, promotions, etc.).

Selling to this segment is the responsibility of the Marketing and Reservations departments of a hotel.

Groups fall into several sub segments: Corporate, Associations (local, regional, national, international), SMERF (Social, Military, Education, Religious, Fraternal), and Banquets. Groups may or may not have hotel-hosted functions attached to their bookings. Most hotels will set a clear number of defined room nights to be considered a group booking, which will be dealt with by the Sales department. Banquets are also part of this segment, but do not always have identified accompanying room nights.

The Group segment is prized by hotels that have meeting space, as this clientele generate revenues at several points of sale throughout the hotel (rooms, food & beverage, spa, rentals, activities, etc.). Group bookings are also obtained through third party planners or site selection companies who act as official agents for company and/or associations that do not have meeting planners within their own organization.

Effective selling to this segment requires a solid set of sales skills. Product knowledge plays a huge role in booking groups. Sales executives must build solid relations with group clients as negotiations tend to take longer and have many more facets to them compared to other segments.

Tour and Travel refers to the Bus Tour and Frequent Independent Travellers (FIT) segments comprised of pre-determined organized bus tours within a country, region or city. This segment usually pre-books large numbers of room blocks in hotels with additional priority access to tourist sights, venues and meal options. Tour companies book a series of dates throughout a particular season and try and use the same hotels as much as possible to negotiate preferred rates. There are two types of tour operators within the Tour and Travel segment. Inbound Tour operators (whose clients are tourists from other countries) or Outbound Tour operators (whose clients are national residents visiting foreign countries). Two types of travel options are usually offered: Group tours that bus clients from tour destination to destination on a set itinerary, or FIT, which has a set individual itinerary but is left to the clients to do the travelling from site to site on their own (by car, plane, bus, train).

Selling to this segment relies heavily on price and inventory, but trusted, long-term client relationships prove a substantial competitive advantage as well. Even though chain-wide negotiations often take place, the local hotel sales executive can make a significant contribution.

Wholesalers are similar in nature to the tour company segment, but act more as resellers of resort destinations. They will pre-buy or guarantee a nightly block of hotel rooms at a discounted rate then sell these same rooms at marked-up rates with an extended package, which may also include airfare and/or activities. Wholesalers deal mostly in resort destinations or high value tourist destinations. (NYC, London, Paris, etc.)

When selling to the Wholesale segment, just as to the Tour and Travel segment, price and inventory are important, but individual hotel sales executives can play a significant role in the sales process. This is a segment that is heavily dependent on well-developed, long-term relationships between clients and hotel sales representatives.

OTAs (Online Travel Agencies) such as Expedia, hotels.com and Priceline made their appearance in the late nineties, and their business model has grown exponentially since.

They are now a major force in the hotel and travel business. OTA's solicit constant room inventory and large commissions (15-30%) from hotels. However they also spend an ever increasing amount of marketing dollars on to the general public and sell an ever increasing number of rooms worldwide. Following several years of misgivings, OTA's and the hotel industry have forged mutually beneficial relationships. Negotiations and inventory control in this segment is managed by the hotel DOS and Reservations.

Crew most often referred to for airline crews business. Airline crews by law must rest for a set amount of time following a flight before they are allowed to take off again on another flight. Hotels accommodate these crew layovers. They are usually based in airport located hotels, however some longer stay required crews (international) will use downtown hotels. Crew rates are generally lower than most other negotiated rates in a hotel and room blocks may fluctuate based on seasonality. Negotiations and inventory control in this segment is usually managed by the hotel DOS and Reservations team.

Where to Find Clients

When you start as a new sales associate in the hospitality business, you will most likely be taking over from someone who has left or moved into another market segment. Here are a few suggestions to immediately put into practice as you begin your new role.

1- If the sales associate you are replacing is still within your organization, **get them to introduce you to as many of the clients that you are inheriting as possible**. Make sure you get properly briefed on each client before you meet them. Knowing their "hot buttons," as well as their concerns ahead of time, will facilitate the transition process and can help you to avoid asking questions they feel you should already know. It does not matter if the client is a big or small in terms of the business they supply - every client wants to feel important and special. You should therefore, allow clients time to get to know you, and make every effort to get to know them. Let me emphasise again - **returning clients are the best type of clients.** They are the least expensive to solicit as far as time and knowledge are concerned and happy returning customers play an important role as advocates for your hotel.

2- If the sales associate you are replacing is not available to brief you - **get on the phone and start booking appointments to meet your new clients ASAP.** You can be sure that your predecessor is not wasting any time in re-soliciting these clients and trying to get them to move over to a new establishment! Again, make sure to properly review any notes you may have on the client BEFORE you meet them. Don't be afraid to ask your colleagues if they have dealt with these clients and what can they tell you about them. You will be surprised by the insight you'll get. Banquet and Front Desk colleagues as well as those in Convention services are privy to the operational side of a client. Information from them can give you the tools to better approach a client in an effective way.

3- **When looking for new clients, ask people you know**. Everyone has friends or family in other businesses. Ask them to put you in contact with the person in their organization who handles group bookings and/or hotel accommodations.

4- **Read the business news**. It is one of the best places to find out who's growing, who's hiring and who's launching something new. Many great leads have been found this way. Most major city and regional news outlets are easily found online. Searching a company's social media sites will also give you the latest news.

5- **Dig deeper into your existing client base**. Upsell and cross-sell. This is often overlooked. Chances are the person you are dealing with in a company isn't the only one able to bring you business. Ask your contact to give you names of others within their organization who may have potential business. What better reference than one coming from a colleague?

6- **Third party planners or destination search firms.** Many companies and/or associations do not always have a department dedicated to meetings. In order to facilitate and organize meetings, companies will turn to specialized planners. Third party planners search out suitable hotel sites on behalf of their clients at home and abroad. Generally these firms have a large array of clients with multiple needs. Identifying these planners, and calling upon them, can bring great results in a short amount of time. Be aware that these types of companies usually require a commission when booking your hotel. These commissions may vary from 10 to 20%, so take this into consideration when quoting rates. Part of these commissions may require payment upfront at the signing of the group contract, so you may be paying far in advance for a booking yet to come.

7- Finding clients **is all about making calls.** It is the optimal way to fill your sales funnel with potential business. You cannot rely on existing clients alone to fill your hotel and/or make your sales goals. Making calls literally means making a phone call or a visit to a client's office. An email correspondence does not qualify as a call. It is too easy for a client to simply delete your email. You will never be able establish a working rapport with a client through email as well as you can with a conversation. You must get on the phone and talk to people. Emails are for follow-ups after an actual discussion. Making calls requires time and patience. Generally you need to make ten to fifteen calls to achieve one successful contact. When the economy is a bit softer this average increases significantly. So again, be patient, put the time in and don't let up.

When using the above principals **keep in mind not to waste time going after business that makes no sense for your establishment.** Discern, through consultation with your DOS and colleagues, who your target clients are. There is no point in pursuing five-star business if you are selling a three- star hotel. The reverse is also true. Chasing business that is unwilling to pay your higher rates is also a waste of time. Take the time to properly identify what types of industries and clients best suit your hotel before you start to cold call potential clients. This is a classic mistake many entry-level sales executives make. In the past, DOSs would tell sales associates to drive to an industrial park and start knocking on doors with the warning, "Don't come back until you have a lead." Looking back, this was such a waste of time and effort. Granted, today's research tools including the web were not at our disposal, so it was harder to find information on companies without literally showing up at the door and interrogating the poor receptionist. Fortunately, selling has morphed into something more strategically planned and organized.

Researching potential clients on the web, and through social media, affords a wealth of information and leads for any and all sales executives. Companies, associations and societies all have pertinent information on their sites, which can be analyzed and used in order to solicit business. Social media is also a great tool to find the right contacts within an organization. LinkedIn, Google +, Facebook, etc. can provide access to the right information you need to make that first call. Plus cross-referencing potential clients on these sites can also lead to several more contacts.

How to Solicit a Client

"Just go out and make some calls," is not what you want to hear from your DOS. Calling on clients is the right idea, but going about it the right way is key. When planning and booking sales calls be prepared and have your goals well planned out. Everyone is pressed for time, so to make productive and fruitful calls follow these steps:

1- The first step in properly soliciting a client is to **get organized and block off time**. Set yourself a weekly schedule with designated time just to solicit and block off all other activities. If you have an office, close your door and ask not to be disturbed. I have seen many successful sales executives actually post a note on their door with a "Do Not Disturb" message while they are making calls. Setting a schedule will help you stay focused and avoid distraction from other issues. Here is an example of a good weekly solicitation routine:

> **Monday** afternoons (2pm to 5pm) call clients from the previous week and to solicit new prospects
> **Tuesday** morning (10am to 12pm) call new clients only
> **Wednesday** afternoon (2pm to 4pm) return calls from Monday and Tuesday and any new clients
> **Thursday** afternoon (2pm to 4pm) return/follow up calls from solicitation earlier in the week
> **Friday** morning (9am to 11am) prepare next week's call lists and return calls.
> **Repeat!**

The rest of the week will be filled with off-site client meetings, site visits, proposal preparations, meetings and reports. It really is a law of averages. **The more clients you speak to and see, the more business you will ultimately have.** A minimum of 70% of your time should be spent on pure solicitation of clients. The other 30% is reserved for research, paperwork, meetings, etc.

2- **Research your client/company before you make the call**. Going in cold and unprepared is a sure fire way to get turned right back out. Clients like to know that you are familiar with their operation and any recent news it may have generated. This knowledge helps to create a conversation and familiar rapport with your client. Most companies, especially publicly traded ones, post a wealth of information on their web sites and social media sites.

3- **Listen, listen some more, ask relevant questions and listen some more.** Yes, you are there to sell clients your product, but if you don't know what they need, how can you properly sell them the right features and benefits? Many junior sales associates feel the need to "feature-dump" everything that the hotel has to offer during their first meeting with the client. It is more important to know which features to emphasise based on what your client has previously told you. This will keep him or her interested in what you have to say. Take your time and have meaningful conversations. Get to know them, find out what their concerns are and about any past experiences positive or negative they have had in a hotel. Listen to what they have to say. Don't sell them something they don't need. **For example,** if your client is interested in booking a one day meeting, he or she will most likely not care if you have a state-of-art spa. If it's just bedrooms they want, they sure do not want to hear about your banquet rooms. If you do a good job and convince a client to book the hotel, you will have plenty more opportunities to promote all the other features of the hotel. **The important aspect is to keep your clients focused on what will win you the business.**

4- Try to **analyse what type of person your client is** when meeting with him or her for the first time. Some clients are very business minded and stay in that mode throughout the call. Others tend to chat more and are friendlier. Some just want to tell you all about themselves and how the company would be lost without them. You may even come across a client who has no clue what he or she wants and are looking to you to help them out. Whatever the type, adjust your sales technique to go along with individual needs. Just be sure to remain professional and courteous in order to get the information that you need to book the business.

5- **Probe for answers.** During your conversation make sure you get the answers you are looking for. Ask your clients for examples if you are not clear on something they've said. Bring a cheat sheet of questions with you to make sure you don't forget anything. Make sure to ask both closed and open-ended questions to best determine what your client really needs. Getting as much information as you can will help you properly bid for the business, and will also enable you to clearly brief the rest of the relevant hotel staff when the booking goes definite. See Annex B for a checklist of sample questions.

6- **Take notes**. If it is written down you will NOT forget it. Clients will also feel their concerns are being seriously considered.

7- **Ask for the business.** If you don't ask, you won't receive. This may seem obvious, but do not underestimate the power of coming right out and asking for the business at the end of a client meeting. Many sales associates leave a client's office without a commitment and then wonder why they didn't get the business later down the road. ASK FOR IT!

8- **Always establish a next step follow up.**
Ultimately, you want to leave a client's office with a commitment. Preferably a booking, but if not, at least a commitment to follow up. Always keep the door open with the goal to attempt to close the business at a later date. Be specific about the nature of and specifics of your follow up and establish a timeline in which to do it. **For example,** confirm that you will send the client a proposal by May 10[th,] OR that you will call the client back in two months to see if they have decided to hold a specific event.

9- **Stay Connected**. It is beneficial to stay connected with clients by sending them relevant information from time to time, on a professional level and also on a personal level if you have built up a comfortable enough relationship with them to know their interests. This creates long-term mutual trust and pays off in future business. **The best clients are those who become advocates for your company through positive interactions at every point of their experience, including with you.**

10- **Be innovative**. Clients are solicited day in and day out. You need to stand out, and above, the pack. Sales associates use all sorts of methods to get a client's attention from sending flowers to gifts. A colleague of mine once sent a St. Bernard plush toy to a client asking her why she was not calling him back – and she did. Another sent a singing telegram to a client, which secured a future meeting. You may not have to resort to employing a gift or stunt, but you must try to think of creative, innovative ways to differentiate yourself and your hotel, while also remaining relevant and pertinent.

11- They say a picture is worth a thousand words, well, **a site inspection is worth a million**. There is no better sales tool than having a client visit and experience your hotel. Seeing is believing. Get your clients to come to you. Breakfast, lunch, dinner, cocktails – anything that you can think of. Any premise to get them to visit your hotel is a good one. Most clients love to be invited for meals or events, so use this inclination to your advantage. I always tell sales associates, "You have it at your disposal - so use it." This is also a fantastic relationship-building opportunity. **Extended face time with clients translates into gathering more pertinent information, trust and lays the foundation for future business.**

31

12- **Be punctual** when getting back to your clients. Always return calls and/or emails in short order, even if you do not away have the answers at hand. If this is the case, inform your client that you are in the process of getting the answer, and let them know when you will be able to address all of their concerns or inquiries. Clients would rather know that the answer is coming than not know what's going on at all. **Poor response time equals lost business**. Always be ten minutes early for any client meeting. This provides ample time to get your thoughts together and assures a punctual arrival if you happen to have a hiccup getting there.

13- **Always thank your client for their time.** As said before, time is precious and acknowledging this fact is always appreciated and demonstrates your professionalism.

14- **The proper handshake.** Make it firm but not overwhelming. Be mindful not to be too aggressive, and always look at the person in the eye when shaking hands.

Landmines to Avoid

Getting to know a client is easier said than done. **Never take anything for granted or make assumptions based on appearance or surroundings.** Here are things to watch out for when initially meeting a client:

1- **Avoid discussions regarding politics and or religion**. I learned this the hard way. I once took for granted, based on a person's appearance and demeanor, that they most likely shared some of the same political leanings as I, and therefore felt comfortable touching on a few political issues. Well, I was dead wrong! Though the meeting ended in a very friendly manner, I later found out that the client was completely at the polar opposite opinion of what I was so confidently pontificating about. Needless to say, I did not get the business.

2- **Be sensitive to cultural differences**. We live in multicultural society with clients from diverse backgrounds. I personally think that we've gone overboard with political correctness, however, cultural sensitivity must be respected and maintained in any client situation. Some cultures are more formal than others. North Americans tend to be rather friendly in their business approach; whereas Europeans and certain Asian cultures are more formal. It is up to you to adjust your sales style to match your client. Researching your clients ahead of time will help you determine your approach and business dealings.

3- **Don't be late**. I repeat myself, but being late is a sure sign of unprofessionalism and disrespect. A professional sales associate should always be at any meeting five to ten minutes early. It demonstrates that you are organized, prepared and respectful of your client's valuable time. If for some reason you will be late, be sure to call ahead to inform your client and apologize.

4- **Be prepared**. Do not show up to any meeting without reviewing your materials and clarifying the reasons for your visit. Doing so shows a total lack of professionalism. Convey a sense of confidence to your client by being prepared and well informed. **First impressions count, and you have one chance to make a positive one that lasts.**

5- **Be mindful about revealing what you know** about your client when you first meet him or her. Social media enables us to gather a huge amount of knowledge on a person. Not every client will appreciate that you have been on his or her Facebook page, so keep things at a professional level until you have developed a closer relationship.

6- **Do not make it "about you"**. The best sales associates put their clients first. There isn't anything wrong in revealing information about yourself, but do NOT upstage your client. Remember it's about booking business, not about your own personal exploits.

7- **Business card etiquette**. One would think the humble business card does not have much place in today's electronic-based business environment, but it is a tool not to be taken lightly. It is still the best way to ensure accurate business contact information. When exchanging business cards, take a moment to read it and acknowledge it. Do not just put it your pocket. If you are in a sit down meeting, leave it on the table in front of you until the meeting is over. In some cultures, such as in parts of Asia, one must present the card with two hands with the type facing the receiver and in return, must be accepted with two hands and read carefully before it is put away. Never play with or fold a business card. This is a sign of disrespect.

Chapter Three – Site Inspections, Trade Shows and FAMs

Site Inspections

Let me begin by recounting my first solo site inspection as a new sales executive three weeks into the job: I meet the client in the lobby and started the tour. We visit a room, the spa, tour the restaurants and all is going well. I finally get to the ballroom and the lights are off. I have no idea where the light switch is. When I finally find a banquet manager and have the lights turned on, the room is a disaster. It hasn't been cleaned from the previous night's event. The client is not impressed, and needless to say, I do not get the business.

From that day forward my site inspections took on a whole new dimension. As I've stated: **A site inspection is worth its weight in gold and there's no better sales tool**. Preparing yourself, and ensuring that the entire hotel is well prepared to host a client for a site inspection makes all the difference to your ability to close the business. If the site is professional and well set up, it sends a clear message to the client that the hotel team is able to efficiently host his or her guests and/or meetings.

Make your site inspections memorable by:

1- **Greeting a client upon arrival**. Get members of the hotel staff involved. Brief the door man/bellmen, so that they can greet the client by name when he or she comes in. Make sure to introduce the client to other members of your team during the tour. Meet the General Manager (GM) if possible. Place a welcome message on the hotels electronic boards. Take a few minutes with your client before you start the tour to go over what you plan to present, as he or she may have specific requests that you can have prepared by other staff members as you conduct the tour, such as setting up a last minute meeting with the banquet manager or the chef.

2- Ask your client how the hotel can **reflect and compliment the expectations** of his or her event. Tailor your site to be able to match and meet these expectations.

3- Make sure to **have the rooms and/or meeting spaces that you plan to visit ready BEFOREHAND** to ensure that no surprises await you as you tour. If presenting a space for a meetings booking, have the room(s) setup in the configuration the client requires or has requested prior to the site if possible. Walk through your site a few hours before your client arrives to make sure all is ready. This will give you time to make any necessary corrections or adjustments.

4- **Add a touch of class** to your site. Have something special prepared ahead of time, such as a chocolate treat, glass of champagne or a small tasting to enjoy during, or at the end of the site. Find out your client's preferences beforehand and have it prepared for them on site, or as a gift to take away. Something that is personalized leaves a much stronger impression than a simple generic offering.

5- **Know the building inside and out**. Be sure to know; where the light switches are located, specific seating capacity, Audio Visual (AV) and staging options, cloak room capacity, access to loading docks, elevator flow and lift capacities, parking spaces, electrical capacities, special needs options, etc. **Ask the right questions to get a comprehensive awareness of everything your client may require for a successful event - and familiarize yourself with anything you are unsure of.**

6- Build **client-specific floor plans**. If you know what your client's meeting space needs are, prepare floor plans ahead of time to review during the site inspection. Do some pre-prep by using easily available meeting specification building tools. This will help you better understand your client's vision and can be mutually adjusted during the site. A small gesture, but one that certainly enhances the appeal and professionalism of your hotel.

7- **Never schedule a site inspection when there is a competitive company meeting in-house**. This shows poor judgement and makes both parties uncomfortable. Furthermore, it may upset the in-house client and jeopardize future business.

Trade Shows

Trade shows are an essential part of the hotel and tourism industry sales process. Gathering a multitude of clients under one roof can translate into a goldmine of leads - or a waste of time if not properly managed. **The take-away is up to you.** There are two types of sales associates at trade shows. Those who remain behind their table/booth and wait for clients to come to them, and those who position themselves in front of their table/booth and approach clients. Guess which type gets more leads? Trade shows are an expensive investment and highly competitive, so don't waste the investment. Effective sales executives view trade shows as opportunities to generate solid leads or close tentative business. Here are a few things you need to know about trade shows:

1- **Prepare your trip**. If you are aware that specific targeted clients will also be attending the same trade show, try to pre-arrange times to meet with them during the show. This is a great way to make sure you make contact. Hoping they come by your booth is wishful thinking. If they do, you may be with another client and you will have missed an important opportunity. Make things happen. Your competition is most likely at the same show going after the same business.

2- **Attend any after-show evening events** either with your brand or with your city CVB. These evening events are a great way to spend time with clients in a more relaxed setting. If there is no event planned, try and organize drinks or a dinner with key clients. There is no better way to build rapport with clients than over a meal. Remember, you are a representative your hotel, so always remain friendly and professional.

3- Get in front of your table or booth. Do not make the clients have to come to you. Get ahead of the game and **initiate the encounter**.

4- **Offer something original** at your booth beyond stress balls and pens. Draw prizes throughout the show; offer a local delicacy or unique experience. Be creative and innovative to set yourself apart from the rest of the competition.

5- Be sure to **take notes**. With a large number of clients coming by and talking to you it's not always easy to remember all the different conversations. Prepare convenient call sheets or access your CRM remotely to help manage the flow of information.

6- Get the **clients' correct contact information.** This will facilitate an effective, timely follow up.

7- **Follow up with clients post-show.** This seems obvious but it's not always done. About 80% percent of trade show leads are never properly pursued. Don't let too much time go by before you re-contact these clients. You can bet your competition will not.

FAMs (Familiarization Trip/Visits)

FAM trips are usually organised by your Tourism Bureau, your company brand, or by your hotel. They are an excellent way to showcase your hotel and your city. Often specific to a particular type of business segment, FAM trips are essentially created to inform potential buyers of your product offering. **Originality and innovation is key to the success of any FAM trip.** You want your clients to leave with an overwhelming sense that they must return with their business. As a junior sales executive, your role in the organization of a FAM is to be part of a team effort. Nevertheless, you can still ensure that the team comes up with an idea that will make your hotel stand out from the rest. Coming up with a theme for the client visit or event at your hotel can be very effective. One overreaching idea makes it easier to get everyone on staff involved and participating in the fun. Put a twist on the site or the event. Make sure the clients remember your hotel apart from the rest.

I once hosted a bureau-initiated city FAM with the theme, "We go bananas over you." I had our GM dressed in a gorilla suit, with the DOS (me) in a banana suit greeting guests as they arrived. The pool area was turned into a beach party and the rooms visited all had theme-related actors and activities. Needless to say, the clients were impressed with the spirit and enthusiasm of our hotel.

The following year we developed a James Bond theme and had the clients participate as spies, with full run of the hotel, with both front and back of the house activities. Again, it left a favourable impression, and helped close some great business.

Chapter Four – The Competition

Knowing your competition is crucial to becoming a successful sales executive. If you want to properly serve your clients as well as win more business you need to know who you are up against. In order to properly analyse your competitors, here are a few things you need to do:

1- **Identify your competition** through a detailed review with your DOS or GM. It is important to physically see your competitors' product. Call your counterpart at other hotels in town and **request a site of his or her hotel**. Plan to go after work hours as a courtesy and so that you will not to take time away from his or her workday (as well as your own). Two things will happen. You will get to see the hotel's infrastructure and you will be able to assess the sales associate that you are selling against. Ask lots of questions, as if you were a client, and listen to the answers. Your counterpart's sales instinct will automatically kick in and you will get a view into your competition's selling style.

2- Study the competitions' building specifications. **Know their hotels as well as**

yours. This enables you to be proactive when a client questions your ability to host their business as compared to your competition. Knowing their limitations could spell success for you. Never be crass or degrade your competitor, nor his or her hotel. Simply and respectfully point out your ability to do, or offer something they can't.

3- If your sales department has not already done so, conduct a competitor **SWOT analysis**. SWOT stands for Strengths, Weaknesses, Opportunities and Threats. List in each one of these categories, attributes, per competitor, and where they stand compared to your product. Be objective. This will give a better idea of what sales angles to take when a client is considering several competitive hotels.

4- **Walk through the lobbies of your competitors' hotels** on a regular basis and check out their reader boards. This is a simple way to acquire future leads. You will not find out who the meeting planner is, but you will certainly know which companies are meeting there. This will help narrow future solicitation efforts.

Chapter Five – Your Partners

The Industry is here to help you. It is important to know that your hotel colleagues are only one element of your success. When considering a hotel, clients weigh several factors into their decision making process. **Brand, location, proximity, service level, price and destination** all play an important role. It's up to you to help facilitate this process for your clients. There are plenty of people who can help. Apart from your own hotel colleagues, several other entities want you to succeed.

1- **Your hotel brand team**. Most brands have dedicated regional, national and even international sales teams scouring their respective territories for business. Chances are, they may know your clients and can help you influence their decisions. They can also be great lead-generators. Get a list of brand sales associates to see who operates in your region or in your segment of activity, and get to know them. Make sure to keep them in mind when it comes time for you to send a lead. In some cases, hotels managed by a third party hotel management company may also have national or regional sales teams. These sales teams maybe even more inclined to find business for you as they have direct accountability with the hotels' owners.

2- **Your local CVB** (Convention and Visitors Bureau). The CVB's very existence is based on its ability to drive business into the city. Some CVBs concentrate on large conventions and/or tour series, but many help out smaller self-contained groups who are considering visiting the city. These city sales associates tend to be ex-hotel sales executives and have a great deal of client and destination knowledge. Make sure to know who they are, and bring them into your sales process when you have clients who need a little extra push deciding what city and hotel is the right fit for them.

3- **Affiliate suppliers**. Audio visual companies, custom brokers, and similar suppliers that your hotel deals with on an exclusive or regular basis can be great assets when trying to close a sale. Depending on whom your client is, and how complex their needs are, know that you can call on these suppliers to clarify any question and concerns that may arise during the sales process.

4- Get to know **other tourism-related players** in your city (Professional Conference Organizers (PCOs), attractions, off-site venues, museums, galleries, restaurants, night clubs, etc.) A good rapport with them can help you win business and benefits how you can best serve your clients.

Chapter Six – Over and Above

We have a saying in the industry. **Make sure to service your client "from booking to billing."** It is easier said than done. Your role as a sales person doesn't stop once the contract has been signed and passed over to the convention services, reservations or the banquet department. You remain the main point of contact for your client. The relationship and trust factor has been built between you and your client, so in his or her mind you remain a partner throughout the process. Granted, you do not want clients to call you endlessly to review menus etc., but you do want them to feel that you are there to protect their interests during their stay or event at your hotel. There is a fine line between you and the Convention or Reservations services point person. It is important not to overstep your involvement in the minutia of client demands, but also important to stay aware of what's going on and look for any potential landmines that may lie ahead. There is one thing you can be sure of, is that if something starts to go wrong the client will be calling you.

One way to improve the service you give to your client is to really know your product offering. I spoke of this in a previous chapter but it worth repeating. Product knowledge is your key to success. **It also**

holds the key to your clients' ultimate satisfaction. A keen awareness of your hotel's full abilities, as well as its limitations, ensures that you will not commit to something that cannot be delivered. I have seen this time and again; sales associates who promise the sun and moon to close the deal, and ruin the chance of future business because of a dissatisfied client. As a sales associate you are responsible in part for the success of your hotels' image, performance and profitability. Therefore it is your duty to go over and above in assuring a premium client experience. Think beyond one simple booking, anticipate concerns and mitigate them, follow the process 'from booking to billing" and ensure the rest of your hotel team is on the same page. All these factors rest, as far as your client is concerned, on your shoulders. **Do not promise what cannot be delivered**. If this becomes the case, social media can become your worst enemy - as I am sure you are aware. Clients have no qualms rating your hotel's poor performance for all to see.

How to Go Over and Above

1- **Study your hotel specifications**, get very familiar with your space capabilities, banquet menus and know what your hotel realistically can and cannot accommodate. With sound knowledge you can properly respond to your client, project confidence and professionalism, as well as help the client make more educated decision on the spot. It will also facilitate the transfer of the booking to your Convention services team.

2- **Understand your hotels' profit margins**. Educate yourself by discerning what is a good piece of business and business you should not pursue.

3- **Know what to recommend** in your city as far as offsite venues, restaurants and attractions. It's not all about your hotel.

4- **Communicate with your colleagues and hotel staff** regarding your clients. There is no such thing as too much information in this business.

5- Do not limit your interaction with clients to hotel-related issues only. Know what their business concerns are, and **get to know your clients on a more personal level** in order to converse on a variety of interests.

6- **Be present when your client(s) are in-house**. Check-in on them at the start, middle, and end of their stay or event. During your post-event visit make sure to gage their satisfaction and if it is favourable, don't be afraid to ask if more business from them is possible. If your client is not onsite or is booking for others, make sure to check-in

regularly for any feedback they may have
received from guests staying with you.

Chapter Seven – Return on Investment (ROI)

Return on investment is something to always keep in mind and understand thoroughly. All investments, whether in people, resources, time, materials etc. are assessed by their profitability based on cost vs. the amount received for the given services or items. In other words, how much did it cost you to get the business compared to the revenue generated from that same business? If the revenues are minimal, or negative, this equates to a bad piece of business. If the opposite is true, that's good business.

A good sales executive is able to calculate the difference. **Knowing what an acceptable ROI is will definitely help you be a better negotiator - and enable you to quickly identify the right type of business for your hotel.** The best way to figure this out for your particular hotel is to understand the business operating costs by department.

1- What is the hotels' **cost of providing a room** per night? One must calculate the housekeeping cost including; labour/housekeeper's time, products used to clean the room, laundry services, heat, lights and power, etc. Your head House Keeper or GM should be able to provide this information, and based on the amount, your DOS or GM will decide the minimum profit margin they expect for that room(s). This will be the difference between the cost of the room and the price you are to charge a client. Profit margins will fluctuate based on time of year and/or yield of the hotel, however, informing yourself of room costs will give you an understanding of the hotels profit margin needs.

2- What is the **acceptable profit margin on food & beverage functions**? Again, cost of the food, kitchen staff, banquet staff, etc., compared to what you will be charging the client.

3- Same thing goes for **AV services, meeting room rentals and all auxiliary services** offered by your hotel.

Understanding your hotel's profit margins gives you the flexibility to better negotiate with your client without always contacting your DOS to make sure what you are quoting is right. **Cutting down the time your client has to wait for answers gets you closer to closing the business ahead of your competitor.** You can also better package your offer by understanding this fact: You may get less revenue in one area, but may be able to make it back in another.

A healthy ROI goes beyond linear lines. You must look at the whole picture. A particular piece of business may seem to be profitable as a stand-alone event for your hotel. However, when analyzing it closely, it may actually pose a huge loss. For example:

1- A small group calls and wants to book a meeting at your hotel. They are willing to pay full rental for meeting rooms, AV, and have breakfast and lunch. Sounds great. They have met all the profit margin criteria. Now look closer. The group wants to meet on a Saturday afternoon and it so happens no other groups are in-house on that date. Banquet waiters will now need to be called in as well as porters to setup the room. The kitchen will need to be geared-up and may require extra staff. All of sudden your margins get smaller and smaller as the event is not big enough to maintain the cost of the staff and resources needed to service it. If the same group had booked during a busier time with hotel staff already in-house, economy of scale, i.e. the ability to spread out the costs over several groups and clients, would have maintained larger margins. **Taking all elements into consideration enlightens your decision making process.**

2- You get a call from a corporate client that has been loyal to your competition for years. They book about a thousand room nights per year of Corporate Individual Travel at one hotel exclusively and are interested in moving their business to your hotel. Sounds like a gift from above, but during the sales probing process you find out that these room night bookings are primarily on Monday, Tuesday and Wednesday, when your hotel is usually already full. You also find out that the price they pay at the competition is as low as you are presently giving to some of your very best clients with larger business volumes. Nevertheless, it is a thousand room nights, and that would help you achieve your sales goals. Is it worth going after this business at a discounted rate knowing that you will most likely be displacing higher paying business and potentially creating availability issues at your hotel on Mondays, Tuesdays and Wednesdays? It seems like a clear choice to turn down the business, and chances are it is the best decision. Nonetheless, in a situation such as this, run the numbers with your DOS and Yield Manager to make sure that there are no other outstanding issues that might warrant the business. Maybe your hotel is about to lose one of its biggest clients and this could replace that loss. Determine if this client may open the door to additional large group bookings within their organization. **Be sure to cover all the bases before you judge a business transaction simply on face value.**

3- An airline sends in a Request For Proposal (RFP) to house Crew arriving from overseas three times per week, year-round. As all airlines, they want a killer rate. Your hotel does really well in occupancy from May to October and slows down significantly November through April. It is obvious that the Crew will be displacing higher paying business in high season. So it doesn't look good so far. However, when you look deeper, the Crew checks-in during the early evenings and checks-out very early the next morning. They stay Tuesday, Friday and Sunday for one night each time. Chances are, if you are an urban hotel, Tuesdays are your only issue in high season as Fridays and Sundays don't usually sell out. Therefore, the Tuesday night displacement in high season might be worth the cost of taking the airline business - even at a low price, to help fill the hotel and bring in revenue on those off-nights and in low season.

Recap; **Don't take anything for granted, always take the time to properly probe for answers, and do the math before you make your final call**.

Chapter Eight – Managing Your Career from the Start

The Hotel and Tourism industry is not for everyone. Be well aware of this before you decide to make it your career. The first thing you need to understand is that it is a cyclical industry which is dictated by the ebb and flows of the economy more than many other industries. **The hospitality industry is the first to feel the effects of an economic down turn and the last to benefit from a recovery**. Why? When companies start to make cuts to maintain their profit and performance levels, they tend, for the most part, to reduce their Travel and Entertainment (T&E) costs. This has a direct correlation to reduction in travel, hotel stays, business meetings, training and client entertainment. When business begins to improve, it usually takes a while for these same companies to open up the T&E tap. As a hotel sales associate, it is in these low times that you must rise to the occasion and maximize any and all revenue for your hotel. The pressure on the Sales Department usually gets turned onto "high" during these periods. ROI margins tend to shrink as the competitive landscape gets tougher and tougher. During these leaner times, you must be at the top of your game, more resilient and sharper than you have ever been. On the opposite side of the coin, when the economy is rolling along, your sales skills are tested in other ways. As demand goes up, it is up to you to find the right and most profitable business for your hotel. This may mean having to say "no" to clients you have had long-term relationships with, and who have been loyal in slower times. An effective sales executive soon learns how to handle both of these situations, while doing his or her upmost to maintain healthy client bonds.

As you have probably ascertained, **this is not a nine to five job!** I cannot stress this point enough. If you want to be a successful sales person in the hospitality business you must put in the time. Don't get me wrong; you are not working in a coal mine. You are however, part of an industry that runs 24/365 all year long. Have you ever noticed that there are no locks on the front doors of hotels? Don't fret; working in this industry truly is fantastic. There is a huge upside to all you will encounter. No day is ever the same, you will meet the most interesting people, your colleagues become like family and if you are in the right market you will travel the world. The remuneration and benefits are also decent. Consider this; you work in an environment that strives to be pleasant and welcoming, making magic moments for your guests. **The fun you will have greatly outweighs any stress you may encounter.**

Managing Up and Across

Managing an effective career means understanding the big picture, just as you would when booking business. **Consider all the elements at play** such as knowing how to manage your colleagues and your superiors. Because you do not have any direct reports, do not be fooled into thinking that you don't have to manage anyone. WRONG! As a new sales executive it is imperative that you create bonds that will help you grow as a professional, and allow you to do your job better. Let me first talk about "managing up": How to interact with your boss and other management team members. Making your DOS's job easier will make your job easier. **Always do what is asked of you in a professional and timely manner.**

1- Have your sales reports in on time
2- Make the weekly calls required
3- Follow up on issues or tasks asked of you without having to be reminded
4- Participate in sales meetings and try to bring value to the discussions
5- Don't be afraid to ask for help
6- Don't wait until it's too late to resolve issues
7- Avoid office politics. They only distract you from you achieving your goals

"Managing across" refers to effectively interacting with colleagues in the Sales Department and in the rest of the hotel. I always tell sales associates that it is vital to work together as a team with their colleagues. Sharing information and doing what's best for the business, rather than what is best for you will always payoff in the long run. There is nothing wrong with trying to get to the mark first, but don't be greedy or selfish about it. **Motivating others, as well as yourself, to work collaboratively will get you much further in your career then doing the opposite**. Get to know the key staff in the hotel that can help you make your clients' experience unforgettable. Do not underestimate how crucial these people are in the equation. You will be happy to have them when the time comes. You are but just one piece of the chain in the entire operation. Remember the following the adage:

Together

Everyone

Achieves

More

As in most industries, **self-motivation plus drive is the key to success**. The vibrant, positive nature of the hospitality business is a driving factor in itself, as you generally work within a strong team environment and have access to other sales professionals for help and whom you can learn from. It's also important to be able to self-motivate. Spending time on the road alone away from home and loved ones can be hard, so maintaining a positive outlook and keeping your focus is crucial.

Management Types

Managers come in all types and all stripes. Throughout your career you will be faced with different types of characters and management styles. As with clients, it is important to be able to identify each style and adjust your interactions accordingly. Some managers are more effective than others, but you must remember that if they are in a managerial role, they're there for a reason and should always command your professionalism and a degree of respect. Some management types you will encounter throughout you career are as follows:

1- **The True and Tried.** These managers have been around for a while, and although they may have had success in the past, they've failed to keep up with the times. They often use phrases like, "If it ain't broke, don't fix it," or, "Already tried that in the past and it didn't work." They are generally not all that open to new ideas and/or risk taking. They tend to stick to a well-regimented plan with a set mode of doing things and are autocratic in general. You can expect to learn the basics from them, but they will most likely not challenge you to go over and above.

2- **The Intense.** I tend to liken these types of managers to sports coaches on steroids. Every issue and conversation turns into a pep talk or an intense play-by-play strategy on how to get the job done. These types of managers tend to be very persuasive in their manner. You will certainly hear a lot of business/sport analogies, receive many lectures, but as a result may not be prone to ask for a lot of help.

3- **All Business.** Some managers are all about getting the job done. They are not so much about team spirit but about team success. These managers are very good at analyzing the issues and making educated business decisions. You will definitely learn about the discipline of the business process and a no-nonsense management style. However, don't expect these managers to be the touchy feely type. Keep things professional at all times.

4- **The Control Freak.** Managers who fall into this type of style tend to be overbearing, lack the element of trust, and must always be in control. They feel the need to be part of every decision and must be aware of all the details involved. This is sometimes because of a lack of self-confidence or mistrust in the ability of others to do the job properly. If you work for a Control Freak make sure to have all your ducks in row before asking for help.

5- **The Democrat.** These types of managers tend to be consultative, encourage you to share your ideas, promote a harmonious team spirit, are big on communication and generally well-balanced in the decision making process. Direction tends to take a little longer, due to the consultative process, but is usually well thought out. Working for this this type of manager means working as a team which is fulfilling and helps to quickly develop your critical thinking skills.

6- **The Laisse-faire.** These types of managers tend to let the Team make their own decisions and get involved only when really necessary. Under this type of management the team usually runs independently and has very little, if any, team spirit. This approach may work well in an environment with very senior executives well-rooted in their jobs, but for a new sales associates, these type of managers are hard to work for, and may be of little help in positively driving one's learning curve.

Should I Move Jobs?

The grass is not always greener on the other side. There is a tendency in the hospitality sales industry for employee transiency. Jumping at a competitor's job offer for a few extra bucks may not always be the right move. It is important, again, to look at the whole picture before making any drastic career move. Make sure to do your homework. Do a SWOT (Strengths, Weaknesses, Opportunities, Threats) analysis on the company that you are considering moving to as you would on a competitor. Investigate their sales team. Is it well-adjusted and do they have a good reputation? Do they work collaboratively or most associates fend for themselves? Is there a high turnover of sales staff? If so, why? Are the DOS and GM the types of managers that you can learn from? I cannot emphasise this enough; **working in a positive environment, where you continue to learn your craft is critical to a successful and fulfilling career.** It will benefit you in so many ways - and can set you up for even greater success.

Investigate who runs and owns the hotel. Brands are very important, but so is ownership. You want to be with a company whose owner has a good reputation for re-investing into the product and keeping it up to par. Some owners prefer to run hotels with minimal re-investment and then sell off the asset. The problem this creates is that as the hotel deteriorates, it gets harder and harder to convince clients to come, making your job increasingly difficult.

You also need to consider any career move based on your potential to impact the business that you will be joining. Will you be able to convince current clients to move over to your new place of work? Will you be going into a different market and have to start from scratch with a new set of clients? Are you upgrading or downgrading in physical property? Even if you are upgrading, it doesn't mean you will be better off. Try not to make any hasty decisions, and do give your current employer a fair chance to get something back from their investment in you. You don't want to become the person who is known for always jumping ship. As a rule, always **give yourself a minimum of two years** in any job before deciding to make a move. Anything less does not give you the time to properly settle in and create bonds within the organisation, as well as begin to establish a solid reputation.

Career Development

Pondering your future and **mapping out a career plan** will help you adjust to, and orient, your working life. Do you want to be a Director of Sales one day? Maybe so, maybe not. Great sales executives don't always make great DOSs. If you love being out with clients, booking business and not having to worry too much about what's going on at the office, you may be better off staying in a sales role. The life of a DOS does have its perks, but it also brings a life of routine. Meetings, reports, personnel issues, team motivation and budget management - these tasks are an everyday reality of the job. It is not for everyone. The up side is that you do get to manage a team, participate in the decision-making process concerning how the hotel is run, and enjoy greater authority in general. It may be too early for you to decide where you want to take your career, but keep the future in mind as you grow within your current role.

It is also important to keep learning outside of the industry. **Cultivate other interests** that have nothing to do with work. A healthy work-life balance is critical in a highly demanding industry such as this. Get away and recharge regularly. Don't be the person who lives to work. Those who do tend to burn and crash at one point. The industry has so much to offer, and life has so much to offer, so be sure to enjoy yourself both in and out of the work place. You will find that respecting and cultivating both areas of your life will only enrich the other.

Take any opportunity for additional training, whether in the form of further sales training within your organization or with any industry-related association. This will enhance your development process. Ask to cross train within the hotel. Spending some time in other client-related departments (banquets, front desk, reservation, etc.) will give you a better appreciation of the guest handling process and the ability to translate that awareness into your own client servicing.

Network within and outside of the industry. Forge as many relationships within the business community as possible. Doing so will accelerate your own growth as a sales executive and may also translate into business opportunities in the future - for you and your organization.

Be transformative. Be an active participant in the innovation of your work and your hotel. Initiate the discussion and don't be afraid to push the boundaries of convention.

Conclusion

I hope this handbook will help you manoeuvre through the first few months of your new career. I believe that if you apply the tips I have outlined, it will help ease any early setbacks, encourage a strong learning curve, and set you well on your way to an exciting career in the hospitality industry.

It's a wonderful industry and I truly wish you every success for your future in it!

Annex A – Quick Reference Checklists

Client Call Solicitation Checklist

- ☐ Conduct brief research on company and client you are about to solicit
- ☐ Check if they have done business with you before (what, when, how much was spent, did they pay on time and is their credit good with the hotel)
- ☐ Ask colleagues if anyone knows the client and get a character description
- ☐ Call client and verify they are still the contact person
- ☐ Confirm if it is a good time to talk. If not, ask when you may call back
- ☐ Have a list of questions you want to ask so you will not forget anything
- ☐ Make sure to get any missing information (contact numbers, titles, addresses, etc.)
- ☐ Take notes
- ☐ Try and book a site, meal, meeting or next step to follow up
- ☐ Thank them for taking the time to speak with you
- ☐ Following the conversation, send an email to confirm next step, and thank them again for their time
- ☐ Update the hotel data bank with information gathered from the call

Site Inspection Checklist

- ☐ Review client's requested specifications and then plan site to showcase these requirements
- ☐ Request Site Inspection rooms from front desk
- ☐ If possible, see bedrooms, or ask head house keeper to do a pre-visit inspection
- ☐ Ensure meeting rooms (if applicable) are clean and set up according to the specifications of the client if possible
- ☐ Brief all relevant staff of the upcoming visit
- ☐ Prepare hotel media kit, any customized plans, and consider providing a small gift for client
- ☐ Greet client promptly at front door at the set time
- ☐ Take a few minutes to review the site inspection plan, and ask if this is acceptable to client
- ☐ Take notes
- ☐ During site inspection make sure to introduce staff along the way
- ☐ Following site inspection take a few minutes to review any concerns, changes or follow ups
- ☐ Thank the client for his/her time
- ☐ Follow up email to client with a summary of site, new offering, confirmation of any adjustments to be made, next steps and thank you
- ☐ Update hotel data bank with information gathered from the site inspection

Trade Show Checklist

- ☐ Book trade show, airline ticket and hotel accommodations in host hotel if possible
- ☐ Plan an additional client event if possible (depending on show schedule)
- ☐ Send emails to prospective clients with an invitation to meet at the show
- ☐ Follow up by phone to confirm time(s) to meet
- ☐ Complete all pre-show preparations
  - ○ Make sure booth, table top is in working order
  - ○ Gather all necessary materials to bring or send ahead by messenger (brochures, business cards, plans, any gifts or related collateral)
- ☐ Once at show make sure to set up well before the show begins
- ☐ Be at your booth at all times and set up rotation with a colleague when you are not
- ☐ Position yourself in front of your booth and be confident and proactive
- ☐ Make sure to get clients' business cards
- ☐ Take notes
- ☐ Post show follow-up
  - ○ Send a personal e-mail to everyone who you met to thank them
  - ○ Follow up directly by phone with those with greatest potential and pursue any leads in the days following the show

- o Update hotel data-bank with all pertinent information gathered
- o Update DOS on results of show and any potential leads

Group Booking Checklist

- ☐ Confirm dates requested and/or alternate dates available
- ☐ Determine the nature of the event
  - o Board meeting, sales meeting, product launch, exhibit, training and educational, open to the public, association convention, social, banquet
- ☐ How often is this event held?
  - o Yearly, monthly, ad-hoc, etc.
- ☐ Get required specifications of group
  - o # of rooms and suites needed
  - o Meeting room set-up requirements
  - o Banquet requirements
  - o AV requirements
  - o Exhibit needs
  - o Special electrical needs
  - o Any need for extended move-in or move-out times
- ☐ Ask for history of group
  - o Where they met before
  - o What time of year they met

- o Number of delegates attended
- o Number of bedrooms blocked and actually consumed
- o Rates they paid
- ☐ Who will be making the room reservations - individuals or rooming list?
- ☐ Arrival and departure patterns
  - o Individual or group arrival/departure
- ☐ Billing information - master bill, individual or a combination?
- ☐ Any VIP requirements (room drops, special requests, etc.)
- ☐ Modes of transportation and/or requirements for delegates
  - o Bus, self-parking, taxi, limo's, shuttles
- ☐ Name of main contact/Decision Maker on site from organization during event
- ☐ Any specific shipping or customs needs
- ☐ Need for any major storage, crates and/or equipment
- ☐ Any required pre/post programing or spouse programs
- ☐ Specific safety and security concerns
- ☐ Any special décor required and if so, what type

Annex B – List of Sample Sales-Probing Questions

For the Corporate IT Segment

☐ Are you looking for an exclusive hotel partnership?

☐ How many rooms/nights on average per year do you estimate you may consider booking at our hotel?

☐ Does your company utilize any additional room/nights within the city?

☐ Tell me about your average traveller and what he/she looks for in a hotel experience.

☐ Is there a booking pattern you have seen with your travellers? If so, what can you tell me about it? (I.e. nights of the week booked, length of stay)

☐ If you are considering us for the first time, what prompted you to look for a new hotel partner?

☐ How do your travellers make their bookings? (I.e. booking window and booking method, direct, through third party, online, etc.)

☐ Would you consider a multi-year agreement?

☐ What rates do you pay at similar hotels?

For the Group Segment

☐ Tell me about the purpose of this event?

☐ What are your preferred event dates?

☐ What are alternate dates you would consider?

☐ Who, and approximately how many are attending this event?

☐ In what other hotels have you held meetings?

☐ Can you describe any issues or challenges encountered in the past when putting on this event?

☐ Is there anything notable from past events that you thought were outstanding?

☐ Are there any special needs required for some of your delegates? (I.e. specific food and beverage, allergies, accessibility, safety & security)

☐ How can our hotel and team make this meeting a success for you?

☐ Are there any other specific requirements for your event that we need to consider?

☐ Does your event require extra time for setting up or tearing down?

☐ What rates did you pay last time you held a similar meeting?

☐ Where have you met in the past?

Annex C – List of Industry Acronyms

AAA- American Automobile Association

AARP – American Association of Retired Persons

Added value – Unique extra services or a commodity offered over and above to entice buyers that are not offered by competitors

Adhoc Group – Usually referred to as a tour group that is not part of a pre-determined series

ADR – Average Daily Rate. Average room revenue of total rooms sold on any given day

ACOM – Association for Convention Operations Management

Ambience – the sensory mood of an environment both physical and in brand "personality"

Amenities – Items, products or services offered in a room or within the hotel

APEX – Accepted Practices Exchange

ASAE – American Society of Association Executives

Apps – Downloadable applications for mobile and/or tablet devises

Bandwidth – Level of frequencies by which an internet signal in carried to a computer

Banquet Manager – Person in a hotel or venue that supervises, coordinates menu plans and all banquet related activities

Banquet Rounds – Round tables used for banquet functions available in several sizes

Benefits Statement – Statement that clearly identifies the attributes that will be of benefit to the client

Booking – A piece of business reserved at your hotel

Booking Pace- Rate at which business is being confirmed by sales department and/or reservations

Booth – Exhibit unit/table with supporting visual and marketing components used in trade shows to promote a business or vendor's offering

Bottom-Up – Selling from the lowest priced items to higher priced items

BT – Business Traveller

Brand – Name and reputation by which a company is known for

Buyer Influence – Aspects of the sale or conversation that entice the buyer (client) to buy a product/hotel/choose destination

CIC – Convention Industry Council

CMP – Certified Meeting Professional (accreditation for meetings industry)

Comp policy – Arrangement for complimentary rooms, meeting rooms, tickets, etc

Covers – Number of meals to be served

CRM – Customer Relations Management

CSAE- Canadian Society of Association Executives

CSM – Convention Services Manager

CTP – Certified Tour Professional

CVB – Convention Visitors' Bureau. Same as DMO

Definite Booking – Confirmed, signed piece of business

Deposit – Partial pre-payment of a service or goods

DMC – Destination Management Company

DMO – Destination Marketing Organization. Same as CVB

Double-Double – A room with two double beds

Double Occupancy – Two people staying in one room and can also refer to pricing by person

Facility – A venue, room, building, physical place

Fact Sheet – A document stating all important top level indicators and facts of any given product or service

F&B – Food and Beverage

FIT – Frequent Independent Traveller. Tour segment term used to describe a self-guided travel program

Fly-Drive Tour – An FIT package that includes both airfare and car rental

Folio – An itemized guest bill from the front desk

Full House – A sold out hotel

Guarantee – The final and exact number of people attending an event

Hot Buttons – Issues or concerns that are of priority to a buyer or seller

HSMAI – Hospitality Sales and Marketing Association International

Incidentals – Charges to an account which are not part of a package or are to be paid individually if not covered by a company

IT – Often used to describe an individual corporate traveller

Market Segments – The distinction between types of business and/or clients (corporate, association, government, 3rd party)

Master Bill – A bill which includes charges for several guests but paid by one entity or organization

Meeting Planner – One who organizes, arranges, coordinates meetings, exhibit and conventions

MPI – Meeting Planners International

Niche Markets – Sub sets of existing markets, more industry-focused market groups (pharmaceutical, aerospace, insurance, etc.)

No Show – Guest that does not show up to calm their reservation and has not cancelled ahead

OTA – Online Travel Agency. i.e. Priceline, Expedia, hotels.com, etc.

Occupancy % - Percentage of sold rooms as compared to total inventory

PAX – Number of people attending

PCMA – Professional Convention Management Association

Post Con – Post convention client meeting to review performance as well as billing, issue resolution, etc.

POS – Point of Sales system used by front desk and reservations

Pre-Con – Pre-convention client meeting to review all aspects of convention with all departments and/or suppliers attending

Prospect – Potential piece of business still under solicitation with no firm commitment

Rack Rate – Highest published room rate in a hotel. Usually indicated on the back of the room door

Red Flags – Items, terms, clauses, attitudes that cause mistrust or negative attention and warn of future problems in a negotiation or business dealing

REVPAR – Revenue Per Available Room. Hotel room revenue divided by entire available room inventory on any given day

RFP – Request for Proposal

Risers – Small elevated platforms often used as non-permanent staging, or to elevate speakers and/or head tables

ROI – Return of Investment

Room inventory – Number of rooms available in a hotel

Round Table Introduction - A term to indicate the time set aside to allow each person in the room to introduce themselves and say a few works

Sales Funnel – The process by which the sales process (steps) leads to the final sale

Selling Styles – The different types of selling profiles and attitudes

Site Inspection – The on site visit by client

Slow Food Movement – Type of cuisine by which local and organic foods are used. Non- processed by mass industrial means. The opposite of fast food

SMERF – Social, Military, Education, Religious, Fraternal segment

Snafu – is a military slang (expression) acronym meaning "Situation Normal: All Fucked Up".

Social Networks – Online web sites where people share information, trends, pictures, etc.

Space Hog – A meeting room configuration that takes up excessive space (U-shape, open square)

SWOT – Strengths, Weaknesses, Opportunities, Threats

Table Top - Usually associated with smaller exhibit displaces used in trade shows

Tentative Booking – Piece of business holding space and/or rooms but not yet confirmed

Third Party Planner- An independent meeting planner or planning company

Top-Down – Usually referred to as selling from the highest rated items down to lesser priced items

Tour Series – Multiple departures to the same location throughout the season

Tour & Travel – Name given to the tour segment. Organized travel itineraries booked through a tour company

Turndown – To prepare a guest room for the evening by re-cleaning room and adding fresh amenities

Upgrade – To accommodate a guest in a superior room or seat at no extra cost

USP – Unique Selling Proposition

UVP – Unique Value Proposition

VIP – Very Important Person

Voucher – A document used for goods and services that have been pre-paid or will be billed later

Yield – The analysis of room sales distribution and price

Annex D: Common Meeting Room Setup Styles

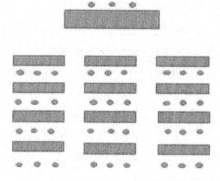

Classroom

Theatre

Hollow Square

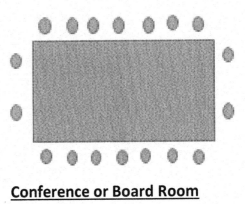

Conference or Board Room

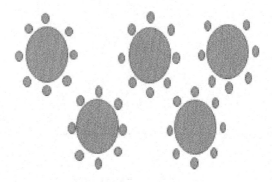

Banquet Rounds

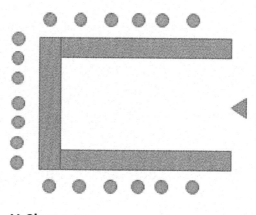

U-Shape

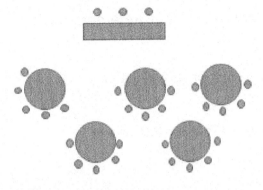

Half Rounds

Annex E: Useful Reference Sites

Professional Associations

World Tourism Organization

www.unwto.org

Hotel Sales & Marketing Association International

www.hsmai.org

Canadian Association of Sales Executives

www.csae.com

American Hotel & Lodging Association

www.ahla.com

Canadian Hotel Association

www.hotelassociation.ca

Hotels, Restaurants and Cafes of Europe Association

www.hotrec.eu

Professional Convention Management Association

www.pcma.org

Meeting Planners International

www.mpiweb.com

American Association of Association Executives

www.asaecenter.org

Association for Convention Operations Management

www.acomonline.org

American Society of Travel Agents

www.asta.org

Convention Industry Council

www.conventionindustry.org

National Tour Association

www.ntaonline.com

United States Tour Operators Association

www.ustoa.com

European Tour Operators Association

www.etoa.org

Global Business Travellers Association

www.gbta.org

European Society of Association Executives

www.esae.org

Asian Association of Hospitality and Tourism

www.asianhto.org

Event sites

Biz Bash

www.bizbash.com

Eventageous

www.eventageous.com

Event Solutions Magazine

www.event-solutions.com

Event Web

www.eventweb.com

Meetings Net

www.meetingsnet.com

Meetings & Conventions

www.meetings-conventions.com

Special Event Magazine

www.specialevents.com

Successful Meetings

www.successfulmeetings.com

Event Marketer

www.eventmarketer.com

Ignite Magazine

www.ignitemag.ca

Smart Meetings

www.smartmeetings.com

Food and Beverage

Epicuraus

www.eat.epicurious.com

Food Arts Magazine

www.foodarts.com

Food Trends

www.foodtrends.com

National Association of Catering Executives

www.nace.net

Wine Spectator

www.winespectator.com

John C. Dunn is President of Dunn Consulting Services Inc. (DCS) a firm specializes in supporting enterprises, small and big, in the travel, tourism, hospitality, events and convention industries. Our focus is enhancing client's strategies and operational plans to increase profitability, manage growth and compete in the world market. John is a 25 year veteran of the tourism and hospitality industry serving as Executive Vice-President of Tourism Montreal, one of North America's most avant-garde destination marketing organizations and as Vice-President of Sales & Marketing for Atlific Hotels & Resorts, Canada's premiere hotel management company, overseeing all sales & marketing strategies for the companies 32 Canadian hotels.

A leading figure in the tourism and hospitality industry, John has lent his expertise to several industry boards such as; the Tourism Industry Association of Canada, The Canadian Hotel Association, The Canadian Society of Association Executives– Quebec chapter, is a founding member of Hospitality Sales & Marketing Association International–Canada Chapter, 1st Vice-President of Destination Marketing Association of Canada and an industry adviser to the Canadian Tourism Commission.

Having worked in close collaboration with the world's leading hotels brands, several destination marketing organizations, convention centre and national and international associations, John has developed a keen understanding of current issues facing the hotel and tourism industry both domestically and internationally.

A native of Sherbrooke, in the beautiful rolling hills region of the Eastern Townships of Québec, Canada, John presently lives in Montreal with his wife and their two children.